BOA
EDITIONS LTD

The Smoke of Horses

The Smoke of Horses

poems by

Charles Rafferty

AMERICAN POETS CONTINUUM SERIES, No. 164

BOA EDITIONS, LTD. ➤ ROCHESTER, NY ➤ 2017

First Edition
17 18 19 20 7 6 5 4 3 2 1

For information about permission to reuse any material from this book, please contact The Permissions Company at www.permissionscompany.com or e-mail permdude@gmail.com.

Publications by BOA Editions, Ltd.—a not-for-profit corporation under section 501 (c) (3) of the United States Internal Revenue Code—are made possible with funds from a variety of sources, including public funds from the Literature Program of the National Endowment for the Arts; the New York State Council on the Arts, a state agency; and the County of Monroe, NY. Private funding sources include the Lannan Foundation for support of the Lannan Translations Selection Series; the Max and Marian Farash Charitable Foundation; the Mary S. Mulligan Charitable Trust; the Rochester AreaCommunity Foundation; the Steeple-Jack Fund; the Ames-Amzalak Memorial Trust in memory of Henry Ames, Semon Amzalak, and Dan Amzalak; and contributions from many individuals nationwide. See Colophon on page 76 for special individual acknowledgments.

Cover Art: *Alphabet* by Colleen Buzzard
Cover Design: Sandy Knight
Interior Design and Composition: Richard Foerster
BOA Logo: Mirko

Library of Congress Cataloging-in-Publication Data

Names: Rafferty, Charles, 1965– author.
Title: The smoke of horses : poems / by Charles Rafferty.
Description: First Edition. | Rochester, NY : BOA Editions Ltd., [2017] |
  Series: American Poets Continuum Series ; no. 164
Identifiers: LCCN 2017010671 (print) | LCCN 2017013552 (ebook) | ISBN
  9781942683483 (eBook) | ISBN 9781942683476
Subjects: | BISAC: POETRY / American / General. | LITERARY COLLECTIONS /
  American / General.
Classification: LCC PS3568.A378 (ebook) | LCC PS3568.A378 A6 2017 (print) |
  DDC 811/.54—dc23
LC record available at https://lccn.loc.gov/2017010671

BOA Editions, Ltd.
250 North Goodman Street, Suite 306
Rochester, NY 14607
www.boaeditions.org
A. Poulin, Jr., Founder (1938–1996)

Contents

For Wendy, Callan, and Chatham

The Smoke of Horses

After the Flood

The day was bright. We saw where the water stopped rising by the marks on the vinyl siding. The raccoons had all come down from their trees, but no one could say where they had gone. On our walk, we found a truck tire welded to the riverbank. The water beside it was a silver ribbon. It was doing its best impression of something that would not chew holes in the railbeds and cover the town with a fine patina of river mud. It was "bucolic," the word the realtors used, convincing us to build here— beneath the trees that never burn, the sky that is ever blue.

Diminution

Socrates taught Plato and Plato taught Aristotle and Aristotle taught Alexander the Great, who founded a city that would house the most voluminous library of the ancient world—until it was burned, until forgetting came back into vogue. The great minds come down through the years like monkeys descending from high branches. Always, a leopard is waiting to greet them—in the tall grass, among the magnetic berries, in the place they should have checked.

Grackles

I have always believed that if I jumped out that window I would turn
into grackles before hitting the sidewalk. Hundreds of them. They would
take off in all directions, and they would not know each other if, weeks
later, they found themselves together on the same telephone wire. It is
not a question of whether remembering or forgetting you is more painful.
It has always been whether I wanted to inhabit those yellow eyes, that
iridescence, that rusty gate of a song that keeps just ahead of your foot-
fall, as you trace the cornfield behind your new house, headed for the
river.

Golf Course Moon

The moon has torn a hole in the weather above my bedroom and is sweeping the dark from my pillow. Wherever you are, I am sure you can see it too, if only you would step to a south-facing window. I remember wanting to shoot a moon like this, to blast it from the sky as if it were a streetlight stuck above the car I was trying to steal. But then I saw how it made your body milk and I drank it from the cup of my coat beneath you, while the stars, dim and without purpose, ground out in the dew of the western grass.

An Adulterous Spring

The sunlight in the leaves is dazzling and wild, sharp as broken vodka bottles. I lean against a blackjack oak, and I swear I can feel the frame of my new bed deep in its trunk, waiting to be let out. The sky is no different—there isn't a cloud to cover up anything. All day the secrets of the world have told themselves, and now you must go back to your husband and your cats, stranding me on this hillside to make sense of these billion leaves, which are really the fingerprints of God as he ransacked the world to find me.

A Demonstration of How One Thing Leads to Another

He steps onto the train and realizes he's missed his stop as he wakes at 40,000 feet above the Andes. He tries to ask the stewardess when they'll land, but by the time he's formulated his question using the English-to-Spanish dictionary he must have packed that morning, he finds himself in the back of a taxicab faltering through Buenos Aires. I'd better phone the office, he thinks, but already he is in the lobby of his favorite brothel being handed a glass of whiskey. Just one couldn't hurt, he says to himself, as he closes the door behind him and turns to see a woman with her dress in a bunch above her waist. He feels suddenly like he's kneeling at the fountain of unquenchable desire. His lips crack painfully even as he quaffs her, over and over, until he wakes inside his wife back in Connecticut, atop their heavy sleigh bed—the one he purchased on credit and a whim, and for which he threw his back out as he hustled it up the stairs.

The Problem with Where We Live

The deer are browsing the topiary as they try to decide which car should kill them. Some nights I'm wakened by the faint snapping of an attic trap, but it doesn't keep me up. Every spring, a cardinal becomes furious with itself in the kitchen window, and our cat collects it from the daffodils struggling out of the garden. We watch him slink into the woods with it, apparently delighted with the way the world is working. This house, I've come to learn, is magnetized for small disasters. The attic never runs out of mice, and the planes slide over like little crosses trying to keep their distance.

Drift

Long ago, the old friends stopped calling. I used to think they had lost my number. Now I forgive them their children and their jobs, their wives and their divorces, their cancer and their lawns, the fifteen minutes they allow themselves at the piano every night. I am able to go on without them—a kind of orphan from the life I used to live. This is what I'm thinking as I get in the car to take my daughter to her voice lesson. The ride is a quiet one. She is getting older and has learned to keep things to herself. When we arrive at the lesson, she makes it clear, without saying so, that I should wait outside. So I stay in the car—doing the bills, doing the things I hate—as her high notes drift through the studio door, the glass of the car window, the air that will be between us now from here until the end.

Mal Evans Counting

You can hear him beneath the orchestral crescendo of "A Day in the Life" as it builds toward mayhem, a small voice counting out the bars as if he were walking through a canyon, going deeper. They needed him to mark out the space where the music would eventually flourish. His voice is winter waiting for a meadow of April glory. It is the dining room table before the dishes and the guests and the mess of a lovely meal. It is your body in the moonlight without a single bite mark—a tiny ghost, a gnat in the air of greatness. It is also a dog tied up in the yard. A boy is throwing rocks at it—24 of them—and the rope is frayed.

Futility

My glances keep hitting her like arrows tipped with moths, marking her with dust she has merely to brush away.

The Man Who Bled Wine

The strange part is that he bled Chardonnay—not the more likely Pinot Noir—and it was cold to boot. He found this out as he was cutting shallots into translucent fingerprints and instinctively sucked out the wound. It was good, so he squeezed his thumb above the nearest wineglass and the bell of it grew foggy. He imagined how women would want him at their parties, a neat little trick by the dessert table, a reason to smack their lips. All night long, he'd hand those women a brimming glass of himself—an invitation to taste what his veins had hidden. He would be dizzy by the end, and he would have to learn to live with it—his concentration suddenly unreliable, like a watch that had been through the wash. He decided it would be best to arrive with bread and cheese, some kind of sliceable meat. Something to keep him going, to stay alert, as they savored the body—the must and the finish—from the cask he had now become.

First Owl

By the time I left her house, the dew was over everything, slick and chill and soaking into my sneakers. I crossed the shortcut field, following the creek that had led me there, wading through goldenrod and half-dead weeds. There was chimney smoke in the air. I kept smelling my fingers, smelling her, as her house got smaller behind me. When I came to the street that would take me home, I looked up to find an owl holding onto a sag of telephone wire. It was watchful and huge, and I was wet to the waist with dew, like a brush dipped into a well of clear paint. The creek beside me crawled into a culvert and under the street. I heard it skipping over the corrugated darkness and thought of rats. When I looked up again, the owl had disappeared.

Reflection

I followed a creek's quarter mile of crashing over rocks and algae and the blurred darting of minnows, until it paused at a pool so well-stopped it looked more like air than water: a sky of contrails, clod-shaped hunks of cumulus. I stepped in and saw the presence of my body disrupt the heavens at my feet. I couldn't find the finches choiring above me, though the branches they must have perched upon doubled there, insisting that stars are possible down here in the earth-hurtle, if only I can wait.

The Problem with Wanting Something

I have been dying under these Connecticut stars all my life, relentlessly, even though the sky is different above Buenos Aires and Lusaka, even though the Magellanic Clouds float like blossoms of dust and could be seen for the price of a plane ticket. In fairness, I have Sirius and Vega and Aldebaran. In fact, most of the brightest stars float above my own backyard as I sip at my palmful of whiskey, so people in the south may feel my pining unfounded. That's the problem with wanting something. Someone will always say you don't deserve it—like lottery winnings or a corner office or a second piece of cake.

Unnoticed

The anniversary of some future sadness passes every day unnoticed. The calendars bear no trace of it; the candles stay in their box. In every house, there's a dead mouse in the wall that the living mice build their nest beside. Meanwhile, it's the usual programs aimed at the sagging couch.

Fitting

The garnet inside this block of schist fits so tightly it cannot be gotten out. The moon that floats like a dime inside this bucket keeps leaking between my fingers. And the decorative bell hanging from the back porch awning has once again filled up with wasps. Look around: The world is glutted with what cannot be removed—the Cabernet stains in your linen shirt, the tumors spilled like pearls along her spine.

The Problem with Sappho

Only one complete poem remains. The rest of it is berries left in the bramble after a visit from midday starlings. For years I couldn't understand how this redaction moved anyone to tears. She was a dampness in the matchbook. But the world is patient. Eventually the diamond travels from the mantle to the finger of the woman you love. Eventually the light from an exploded star arrives to confirm the emperor's power. It's clear now that a very old bruise can tell us how hard someone was punched. The detective solves a murder by the help of a single hair. Archaeologists find a molar and build a face to fit.

Attraction

She collected men the way a light left on collected bugs. It was an old story—money, gravity, the right amount of cleavage. And yet the most successful root never stops fleeing the seed where it began. The cars of two drunks decide to kiss, the lit match gives in to the windy field. Here's a lesson: When people heard there was an albino deer in the woods behind our house, they set out the apples and corn. The shotgun pellets stuck in our tree go deeper year by year.

Insomnolence

I navigate the dark house by moving from the green star of the smoke detector to the blue star of the electric toothbrush. I am no different than Magellan or Marco Polo, I am guided by what burns. Some nights I step onto the back porch. The prow of it charges the blackness, while the stars above me sharpen and blur. Inside, I harbor the ache of what is no longer possible.

State of Affairs

The pond we kissed beside was full of soda cans and stars. The bathroom sink continues to drip into the orange stain of itself. The same color would be pleasing in a moth. Here's something I've learned: The more birds, the more likely they will leave a tree at the same moment. Numbers induce order. The daylily opens three petals at a time. It doesn't care which bee crawls in.

Flags

Some people hang up flags of countries I could never name. Even so, the same colors recur; rectangles and stripes predominate. It's a wonder that Hungary and Bulgaria can tell each other apart. Stars are nice, but they become monotonous—I long for one that is green and thirteen-pointed, with a gentian in the center. Incredibly, not one of the world's flags has polka dots. Why do we bother with passports—their signatures and fees? Wherever we sleep, the same clouds drift away.

Genie

He thought the sudden polishing of the shirt sleeve would be his redemption. After all, it had been centuries since he'd even heard a footfall on the drip-slick stone of the cave. But there he was, tethered to his lamp like a stubborn flame, refusing the million dollars, the bigger dick, the three more wishes. Caught between the cramped brass and our monumental pettiness, the genie couldn't bear to fully enter a world in which desire could reach no higher than a cookie jar.

Metropolitan

In the evening, we got high on the roof and saw the people and the cars pulsing eight stories below us. The scene never repeated itself, and in the air above us, always at least three planes. Our friend who was missing, who was living on the edge of a desert in Mauritania, had written that there were never planes, that the people in his village would not believe him when he said the slow-moving lights were satellites. Their skyline was dung fires and lanterns. They ran a projector off a car battery and watched old cartoons on somebody's bedsheet pulled taut across a wire. Here, the light was careless. The rooms remained lit even when no one was coming back. If we stayed on that roof long enough, the city would fully ignite. We understood how people could be drawn to it over a great distance, how things accrete, accumulate. It was like an avalanche moving down a mountain, getting larger as it went, but made of light. Each night it came down on us like a glittering disaster. We passed the joint. We uncapped the bottle. Even if we ran, we would still be in its path.

The Problem with African Violets

African violets are the lapdogs of flowers. They cannot live outside. Not up here anyway, where the snow is so garrulous, like my grandfather after his morning highball. We would like to touch the fake-looking depth of their petals, but they won't let us—they break or bruise. Even drops of water left on the leaves will damage them. Think about that—a flower destroyed by water. It's no different than chihuahuas and toy poodles: They put on a sweater to take a piss, the wrong kind of food makes a mess behind the couch. Give me the deep-rooted weeds of the yard. Just ignoring them brings them to flower. No one knows their names. No one pays money to fill the grass with them. No one catalogs the exact shade of blue that stutters out of the ground like commas. In a week they're gone, of their own accord. My grandfather, if he were alive, would tell me nothing beautiful belongs to us. As soon as we name a piece of the world, we tame it. We take its power. We cut off its balls and give it a sweater.

Winter Festival

The driveway is too deep to be shoveled. At a time like this, you learn what can be done with mustard and flour and martini olives, and in the first days, you have the feeling you could keep it up for weeks. The season holds fast like a grocery bag caught in somebody's chain-link. Now and then, there is the brief cracking of another barn roof giving in. You wait for the snowplow to clear a path to the liquor store, as the salt eats into the mortar of your porch and the hawk stays pinned like a boutonnière to the branch above the feeder. You haven't filled it, but the finches come to check on it at dusk as the lights of the prison, on the opposite hill, tremble in the trees—like the stars you once made love beneath and to which you hearken back.

Leisure

The darkness takes refuge beneath our bed again, and it doesn't matter that the sun has risen a minute sooner than it did the day before. We have curated a warmth merely by lying here, and we take turns hitting the snooze button. The dog has not complained. The birds will not die down. We wait for the eggs to cook themselves.

Caught

After we made love in your second-story apartment, I saw the plastic grocery bag caught in the branches outside your bedroom window. Six months later the bag was still there. You were a clean person—you didn't tolerate dust on the piano or crumbs underneath the toaster. I told you I could grab it with a broom handle without much effort. At the very least, I was sure I could park it in front of somebody else's view. But you said you liked the sound of it in the breeze, that it was an urban wind chime. That bag was the same shade of skin as your belly when you'd been ravished by the sun. It was the color of a cookie you fed me once when I wanted something else. "Leave it alone," you reasoned. "You never see a tree with two bags in it. Taking it down invites another—possibly more hideous and out of reach." That was the moment. That's when I knew I could never leave.

Two Pianos

The pianos from two different ballet studios have blended together. They are the same key and tempo, and I am equidistant between the open doors, waiting for my daughter to finish up in the studio to the left. This new song is both familiar and unpredictable—like the weather in April or the body of my wife in bed—and the girls in both rooms are dancing to it. Strange how the world stitches together sometimes. We graft the mimosa branch to the maple trunk, and it decides to hold. Almost every Saturday night somewhere, a drunk teenager's heart is sewn inside an old man. The sky does something incredible, and every puddle repeats it. Behind me in the plate-glass windows, the daylilies race like slow fire over the hills of the town landfill.

Two People Kissing in the Park as Seen from a Speeding Train

The moon was a dirty dish above their kissing. The cherries on the branches could not be seen, but they were full of worms and pecked-out holes. If it were the sun above them instead of the moon, they would know that the grass was deeply green. Of course, it had been misted by poison all summer. It was that kind of story. The deer ate the grass. The birds ate the cherries. The man and the woman kept kissing. From a distance, they looked like they were devouring each other and finding the meal delicious.

Windows

Their clarity implies that we can look through them with ease from either side. In truth, we'd eventually be arrested for looking in, and the people looking out see only a panorama of things they cannot touch. This is what I thought about as I orbited your block all those years ago. You sat at your window inhaling the night, but a neighbor and a streetlight held me back. I couldn't get close enough to see your eyes, to tell if I was a part of the world you wanted to come inside.

For the Last Polaroid

Nothing says love like amateur porn. The photographer will position the woman on the bed or the chaise lounge, telling her to open wide, to give him the face of ecstasy. After, they will stand together watching her body resolve like somebody creeping through fog towards them. The woman will be embarrassed, but the man will say it's perfect. And that will be the end, like so many others—the last arrowhead chipped out of flint, the last stagecoach hooked up behind a horse. And then it goes into the keepsake box—the one they hide from their children, the one they must burn before they die.

Aqueduct

Something makes you think of her and a toppled aqueduct at the same
moment—the kind that is found by accident, as when a road is being
excavated in some Italian village and the men step down from their
giant machines, gazing into the dirt as they try to make sense of the
pattern in the stones. Someone from the university will tell them they
once carried water to the mouths of men. It will be hard to believe. It
will be harder to refute. And the machines will all lie idle long after the
new men arrive with their tiny brushes and unmotorized tools, their
theory of the dirt you stand upon.

Quarry

Someone carted off the mountain using dynamite and metal claws and trucks so big the driver needed a ladder to get inside. And then it filled with water—a square lake that went so deep you could have a conversation as the flung penny descended. Every few years a kid from the high school drowned in it, which is why there was a chain-link fence and why it was twisted open by the wild roses. It looked like slate, so I imagined that mountain had been converted to patios and custom rooftops. When we partied there, we tossed our empty Rolling Rocks in without fear of future stitches, and we knew what the bottom must look like—a layer of beer-bottle green accreting to form a band in some future metamorphic ripple of the earth: Stone of hope. Stone of boredom and despair. Stone of barrel fires and taken virginity. Stone that made a space for us beneath the mediocre stars. Stone of a mountain mostly missing.

The Reductionist

The girl who kissed me first never kissed me again. It's as if I spat her out across the years, farther and farther, until the taste of her disappeared, until she was reduced to black ink on an ivory page. More and more things are ending up this way: mountain ranges, the cosmos of swamp water, the wind as it rolls across ripening hay—all of it rendered in a tiny font that shivers like ants beneath your breath, leaving the worm exposed.

Resumption

The snow has become indistinguishable from the street it used to smother. The dog shits of winter have reemerged. Everything hidden returns in force. I should know that by now. Each flower, damp and pushing toward light, prepares the note of its hollering. It won't be long before the bridesmaids are spilling drinks upon their dresses, before I'm smashing the mole tunnels flat.

Royalty

The dew across the lawn is sparkling like a smashed tiara. The trees are filling with a bird confusion. This is our coronation. We must greet it now, embrace it. You will not have left me if I can reach you before the entire tower is cast in light. That's the kind of pronouncement I like to make. Thus, I am wading into the moat, heading for the spot where the stones have formed a fingerhold. The mud is black, and the crocodiles haven't eaten in weeks. The terrible light crawls down to me as if it were a blade.

Barbarian

After the invaders entered the palace, they dragged the great tapestries down. They cut them apart as they called for beer, and the queen was made to serve them without taking off her crown. Later, she gathered up the scraps and took them to the stables so that she might end the shivering of her enemies' horses.

Garden State Racetrack

When I was ten, the grandstand burned to the ground in the next town over. The black smoke galloped into the air right over our house, and ash the size of silver dollars began landing on the lawn. Later, when we heard what happened, we believed it was the smoke of horses, the smoke of our drunk fathers, the smoke of the money that would not feed us. I remember that the ash dissolved when I picked it up, that I had to scrub my hands twice to get rid of it. The following morning we would ride our bikes to make certain what had burned.

The Problem with Mercy

At 2 a.m., the dog nosed up a robin on the pavement beside my car. It was less than a fledgling, and the nest was high above us in a parking lot paper birch, its fist of twigs and threaded trash plain in the August lamplight. It wasn't clear whether the bird had fallen or been nudged out by its cruel and practical mother. The robin would die, I could see that. The ants had already found it like a dropped sandwich, and they were excavating some part of it from underneath. So I raised my boot and brought it down, and felt all its small bones burst. The dog was determined and had to be dragged away. Back inside I poured myself a drink, believing I was right but knowing I couldn't say so, and I was relieved when you weren't awake to ask me where I'd been.

Blackbirds

It was an April morning, full of fog, the sun just heating up. All around him hundreds of blackbirds went crazy in the full surging of their song—red-winged, fluttering, and dark. They kept thronging into his path as if they were weaving something more substantial than their own joy. They snatched at cattails that bent beneath them—they shrieked, they disappeared. In another year, he would know the difference between marsh and swamp. He would learn the name of the orange flower that opened every August behind his house. He would meet the girl that he would marry at a party gone loud and smoky, and when they kissed by the moon-enlivened lake, the taste of her touch said blackbirds.

Hotel Bible

I cannot count on you as I do the supply of tiny soaps, the list of local restaurants. Your message is too small, almost invisible in this dinnertime light. My suitcase is waiting on the bed, still unopened, filled with the little stacks of my button-downs and pants. On the end table, the phone is the color of cave air in its cradle of dead bells. When I drop you down and go to the window, the street below is full of the emptying city. The sun, in decline, sets itself off like a bomb in the disordered closet of the clouds. Back on the writing desk, beside the complimentary pen and the untasted lip of the water glass, you are open to the page where someone paused—your binding cracked to mark the place of salvation or surrender.

Catena

If you look hard enough, you can see how da Vinci made Pollock inevitable. It has never been otherwise. We share 15% of our genes with mustard grass. You can see how a swamp becomes coal and then stack exhaust and finally a melting continent. Medieval man used to believe in a great chain of being—a series of unbreakable links connecting the lowest insect to the dogs and serfs of the world, all the way up to the bishops and the kings, with the last link fused to the gown of God—his fingers on fire and welded to pain, trying to unhitch himself from that which so many desire.

The Problem with Spotfin Shiners

They live their entire lives with the same expression. It doesn't matter if they are hiding or fucking or shooting like spilled marbles into the deeper pools. For them, the dream of flight is suicide, as is the dream of floating in one place with scales the color of a bitten moon. It is almost a curse, how their bodies are all receptor, a brilliant nerve. Even as they are being devoured, they cannot close their eyes.

Magellan

He gets credit for being the first to circumnavigate the planet. The truth is he died in the Philippines with half the trip still ahead of him, after trying to kill some natives who refused his Christianity. I say he doesn't deserve the Wikipedia page. Give all the glory to Elcano. Rename the Straits and the Magellanic Clouds. Would we cheer the man who kicked a sixty-yard field goal if it only made it to the twenty-yard line? By the same logic, the Wright brothers landed on the moon, and I lost my virginity on the way to high school biology when the halls were crowded one day after third period, allowing me to graze the angora triceps of Stephanie Stiles—the only time I touched her in all those heaving years.

Antique

The past pursues you like a great-grandmother's sideboard, from one generation to the next. Let's say that you were thoughtless enough to go it alone, to drag it to the curb with the week's trash. Somebody would rescue it. The sideboard would continue into the future in someone else's dining room. The world will not let go of its junk, and you might as well keep it close. Even now, I'm told, every breath I draw contains some atoms that Jesus once breathed, and a little bit more of them from Hitler and Reagan. Will you be able to bear the face of your mother when she learns what you have done? Can you keep a steady hand as you ladle out the soup from the bone-white tureen so many before you have not let fall to a kitchen floor?

An Explanation of How One Thing Leads to Another

He has climbed so high into the maple tree that he's afraid to shinny back. He calls and calls but it is winter, and the windows of the houses around him are shut. Night has fallen as well, and thus the family next door has no chance of seeing him wave as if their ham dinner were a rescue plane flying just to the north of his desert island, where there is no airfield and the natives would destroy whatever landed anyway, because they believe it is the spirit of their ancestors descending from the sky. After all, what good are spirits if they cannot be dismantled into pieces so small they can be cherished and carried home and kept in a special place, until at last they are forgotten and the relics thrown out like so much bric-a-brac? Here's a proof: The only thing I have belonging to my great-grandfather is a large Irish penny worn almost to the point of not being money.

Proofs

The hailstorm that whitened the lawn became an August dampness. The salt shaker I thought was empty had a serving inside the cap threads. And look, the cicada shell is stuck to the fence by way of explanation for the song above my yard. I remember the impression you left in the living room chair, the mess you made of the Sunday paper with your coffee rings and reckless folds. Quite likely, it is some of your hair that is clogging my bathroom drain. I want you to know your number stayed in my book—even after you married, even after you died.

The Untuned Piano

The wires go slack at different rates until my favorite song sounds as though I'm staring at a beautiful woman with somebody else's glasses. The room in which it waits has been arranged: There is a white rug that makes me worry about my Cabernet, there is a grandfather clock that loses a minute every two weeks, and there is an old map of Europe, the year of which is 1750. Almost none of the countries remain on the map, and those that do have bled beyond the borders I have always known. The piano has become something I have to dust, and my reflection in the wood makes me think of being underwater—the blurry depths, the discordant breath of the risen. Still, it will always be the perfect place for a vase of flowers, no matter their state of freshness.

Pelican

The pelican lived inside her thigh. She would take it out at nights and place it on her bureau, watching it preen the blood from its feathers, happy for the space she made for it among the necklace trees, the kiss-marked photos of the man who left. Each morning, she had to coax it, like a second femur, back into its hiding place. At work, they handed her the forms and she filled them in. She could feel the pelican shifting, ruffling in place, impatient for the promise she could not keep.

Ellipses

You leave out the boring stuff. With you, it's all car chases and sex scenes. You are three gunshots squeezed off in the distance, surrounded by silence and the expectation of sirens. You depart the page like an echo, like the last of the snow converting to mud, like the three birds that lifted off their wire and flew away from me this morning, as if the matter could be settled so easily. You are three ants threading my yard in search of the perfect crumb. You are the belt of Orion. You are the redaction, the burned love letter, the knock of the bill collector. You are three darts thrown over a cliff in search of the lurching sea . . .

Forecast

Famous people have been dying all week, and the Christmas tree just stopped drinking. Talk about omens. It's impossible to get the venetian blinds to stay level anymore. Everywhere I look, people are running the errands they won't remember by this time tomorrow. I remember how, years ago, I had to cut the fishing line caught in the high branches beside the Mullica River, sacrificing the lure that put a kink in my neck as I hunched over my own lap to tie it. I fear my wife will decide to spend my last decade on earth with a better man. I fear I'll be a footnote to somebody else's grandeur. I fear I'll die as painfully as I deserve. One by one, the bulbs of the chandelier go dead above our dining room table. I wish I could say the coming dark was taking me by surprise.

Summer 1985

That was the season I wrote everything in Lucida, instead of Times New Roman. There were no planets in the sky whenever I thought to look for them, and I kept in my wallet a picture of the girl I thought I'd marry behind a picture of the girl I was with. By July, the caterpillars had eaten every tree in town, but they releafed in August, and it was strange to see that shade of new green edging the backyard thunderstorms. I looked through a bell of cheap Chardonnay and saw the world distorted, exactly as it was. At some point, I chipped my tooth on a peach pit but didn't have the money to fix it. It's at home on me now—like the scar from my smallpox vaccination, or the sweater I kept by accident after a host had loaned it to me when he learned that I was cold.

Snowfall After Hearing Hard News

You had your extra socks, your reasons to step out into it, and so you did—deep into the woods, following the turns of a frozen creek, until at last you arrived at a stone wall smothered by what fell. It used to tell where something ended, and your voice was different there. Hours passed. The sky shifted from the gray of your grandfather's overcoat to a shoal of shattered oyster shells. The footprints that took you there had all but disappeared when you began the long trudge back. The birds said nothing, and it happened so long ago. Can you believe you thought the place you came from would be the same place you'd return?

On First Looking into Keats's Chapman's Homer

With a title like that, it makes you think about the canon, how we're all holding to the light the same few moments, trying to pick up a glimmer someone hasn't seen before. *Death scares me* has already been covered, as has *I know a woman who's beautiful* and *Death is a tonic if I can't have the aforementioned beautiful woman.* It's all quite repetitious—like one mirror looking into another mirror looking back at the other and so forth. It makes me wonder if someday somebody will write a poem called "On First Looking into Rafferty's Keats's Chapman's Homer" and whether they still won't care about the confusion of Cortez for Balboa. Some lies just sound too good to be corrected—like *God has a plan* and *I'm certain she's coming back.*

A Farewell to Poetry

Push a dead dog to the bottom of your well. Set fire to the fields on the night before harvest. This is the big goodbye. It is time to blow out the stars. Look at your bills, listen for your name at cocktail parties. Think of the women who took your poems and never undid so much as a button.

The Saddest Bid for Immortality Ever Devised

I used to transcribe my poems on the blank pages of books by famous poets. I imagined they would ride into the future like remoras suckered to the belly of a powerful shark. But the librarian would always find them and black them out. Later, she resorted to excising the vandalized pages with a ruler and a blade. Those stubs at the end of *Paradise Lost* in the Mount Laurel Public Library? That's me.

Acknowledgments

A Lonely Riot: "Carp";

American Chordata: "Fitting";

Bridge Eight: "Snowfall After Hearing Hard News," "The Problem with Where We Live";

Cincinnati Review: "Antique," "Leisure," "Quarry";

Connecticut River Review: "On First Looking into Keats's Chapman's Homer," "Two People Kissing in the Park as Seen from a Speeding Train," "Windows";

Diaphanous: "Ellipses," "The Untuned Piano";

Hamilton Stone Review: "Genie";

Per Contra: "Summer 1985";

Ploughshares: "The Problem with Mercy," "The Problem with Wanting Something," "Unnoticed";

Plume: "The Problem with African Violets";

Poetry Daily: "Leisure";

Rabbit Catastrophe: "First Owl";

Rattle: "The Reductionist";

Salamander: "State of Affairs";

Scapegoat: "Royalty";

Storyacious: "Drift," "Flags";

Tallow Eider Quarterly: "Pelican";

The McNeese Review: "Mal Evans Counting";

The New Yorker: "Attraction," "Diminution," "Forecast," "The Problem with Sappho";

Theodate: "Hotel Bible";

The Southern Review: "A Demonstration of How One Thing Leads to Another," "After the Flood," "An Adulterous Spring," "An Explanation of How One Thing Leads to Another," "Blackbirds," "Caught," "Golf Course Moon," "Insomnolence," "Metropolitan," "Resumption," "The Saddest Bid for Immortality Ever Devised," "Two Pianos," "Winter Festival."

Some of these poems appeared in *Diminution*, a chapbook published by Paper Nautilus Press.

Many thanks to BJ Ward for his close attention to these poems.

About the Author

Charles Rafferty is the author of twelve poetry collections. He has received grants from the National Endowment for the Arts and the Connecticut Commission on Culture & Tourism, and he is the winner of the Nano Fiction Prize, the *River Styx* International Poetry Contest, and the Robinson Jeffers Tor House Prize in Poetry. His collection of short fiction is *Saturday Night at Magellan's*. Rafferty's work has appeared in such places as *The New Yorker, O, Oprah Magazine, The Southern Review, TriQuarterly, DoubleTake, Louisiana Literature, Prairie Schooner, Quarterly West, Massachusetts Review, Poetry Daily, Verse Daily, Per Contra,* and *Ploughshares*. By day, he works for an information technology research company, and by night, he directs the MFA program at Albertus Magnus College and teaches at the Westport Writers' Workshop. He is an amateur archaeologist and a student of many musical instruments. He lives in Connecticut with his wife and two daughters.

BOA Editions, Ltd., American Poets Continuum Series

Colophon

BOA Editions, Ltd., a not-for-profit publisher of poetry and other literary works, fosters readership and appreciation of contemporary literature. By identifying, cultivating, and publishing both new and established poets and selecting authors of unique literary talent, BOA brings high-quality literature to the public. Support for this effort comes from the sale of its publications, grant funding, and private donations.

The publication of this book is made possible, in part, by the support of the following individuals:

Anonymous x 3
Alva H. Angle, *in memory of George M. Angle*
Christopher & DeAnna Cebula
Gwen & Gary Conners
Susan DeWitt Davie
Maria & Joseph Finetti, *in memory of John Finetti*
Gouvernet Arts Fund
Peg Heminway, *in honor of Grant Holcomb*
Sandi Henschel
Christopher Kennedy
X. J. & Dorothy M. Kennedy
Boo Poulin
Deborah Ronnen & Sherman Levey
Steven O. Russell & Phyllis Rifkin-Russell
Sue Stewart, *in memory of Stephen L. Raymond*
Bernadette Weaver-Catalana

Printed in the USA
CPSIA information can be obtained
at www.ICGtesting.com
JSHW082225140824
68134JS00015B/736